The Art of Dissolving

poems by

Donald Illich

Finishing Line Press
Georgetown, Kentucky

The Art of Dissolving

Copyright © 2016 by Donald Illich
ISBN 978-1-63534-045-7 First Edition
All rights reserved under International and Pan-American Copyright Conventions.
No part of this book may be reproduced in any manner whatsoever without written permission from the publisher, except in the case of brief quotations embodied in critical articles and reviews.

ACKNOWLEDGMENTS

I am grateful to the editors of the publications in which the following poems first appeared:

Blue Fifth Review: "The Same Stars"
Crab Creek Review: "Celestial Strut"
Drunken Boat: "The Creation"
Free State Review: "The Art of Dissolving"
The Innisfree Poetry Journal: "The Moon Is Up"
JMWW: "Reservoir"
Moon City Review: "Misdirection"
Open Letters Monthly: "Words"
Pink Line Project: "We Tried to Surrender to the Bus Driver"
REAL: "Road, Sky"
Redactions: "Surgery"
Red Omnivore Review: "Factory Voice"
Steel Toe Review: "How the Moose Fell in Snow"
The St. Petersburg Review: "The Morning of the Scissors," "When She's Out"
TAB: "Hail Music"
Two Weeks: A Digital Anthology of Contemporary Poetry: "The Universe"
"Gravity" is forthcoming in *Gargoyle*.

Publisher: Leah Maines

Editor: Christen Kincaid

Cover Art: Julia Berzhanskaya

Author Photo: Julia Berzhanskaya

Cover Design: Elizabeth Maines

Printed in the USA on acid-free paper.
Order online: www.finishinglinepress.com
    also available on amazon.com

Author inquiries and mail orders:
Finishing Line Press
P. O. Box 1626
Georgetown, Kentucky 40324
U. S. A.

Table of Contents

Gravity 1
Factory Voice 2
The Same Stars 3
The Creation 4
Words 5
House 6
All That Happened 7
Road, Sky 8
The Moon Is Up 9
The Universe 10
Hail Music 11
Reservoir 12
Surgery 13
We Tried to Surrender to the Bus Driver 14
Jeff 15
The Morning of the Scissors 17
How the Moose Fell in Snow 18
When She's Out 19
Horses 20
Celestial Strut 21
The Team 22
The Art of Dissolving 24
Misdirection 25

For my parents and Julia

Gravity

My parents used to tell me
that gravity turned off at night.
That everyone floated
in their nightclothes, bouncing
against the walls of their rooms,
sometimes flying out a window.
When someone woke up, like me,
everyone returned to their original
positions, snoring as if nothing
had happened. I don't know why
they told me this, except to screw
around with my imagination, to keep it
working in a useless direction.
Even now, at three in the morning,
I try to catch my wife hovering
near me, with the books and shelves
above us, bobbing near the ceiling.
I sometimes have the feeling
I was the one whom gravity abandoned.
That I'm the loose person, who will
stick to neither a job or a life.
No one tells me, though. They
watch me rise like a balloon,
sending darts toward me, waiting.

Factory Voice

In my house I speak in a factory voice
above the dinner clatter, loud enough
to resist the heavy metal stereo, big

and bright like the shiny silver fridge.
I command all of you to eat as one,
slurp spaghetti at the same time, exit

seats and enter the lawn, raking leaves
with the same motion, making them
into equal piles of orange and red.

With my words I summon you to bed,
where the sky is blue-black, the window's
screen shaves stars from the rooms.

Only when you are all sleep, tunneling
to places where there's quiet, do I decide
to modulate my volume. My lover only

likes me when I'm a whisper, when
I tell her how I adore her so silently
that only she receives the message.

The Same Stars

This time life didn't get it right.
I woke up in the morning to the same
stars of yesterday. Pots and pans
in their old positions by the sink
instead of in the cupboard. My lover
alive and singing to the Velvet
Underground, and not being prayed on,
in the morgue. I thought I could change
what happened, if I moved a pan
to a different place her blood vessels
would not burst inside her head.
But I realized she was not something
I could undo. She insisted on taking
the stairs. She refused to let me
drag her away. And when I ran up,
out of breath, her body a last memory,
I found her again, lost to this world.
I asked the clouds if they'd alter,
if that would change her fate. I told
the phone to ring, the TV to turn off,
the sun to glow a little less. Nothing
listened to me. I would go back
to sleep later on, wondering why she
hugged me this day, why she was
the one who worried. Why my left side
stung, and why I was buried in dreams,
with the same stars lit above me.

The Creation

At first we were stones, thrown over the backs
of the flood's survivors. When we revealed arms,
sprouted legs, we could see what animals were
talking about: the rush of sensations, the burst
of need for warmth vs. cold. No more hardness
except in our future ways toward one another,
when the world grew older, and many deaths
had chased enthusiasm away. At the beginning,
though, even the sun was a surprise, a face
laughing with us instead of mocking our lives.
The sky gave us rain, which we applauded,
as if an audience happy with everything it saw.
Lying on our backs, did we know the facts
would pick us up, throw us around, a cyclone
with a milky white center of decay? Oh, pretty
skin, oh, beautiful teeth. Until then we loved them.
Our sweet and simple flesh, alert, eager eyes.

Words

When I wake words want me.
Sleep wishes to drag me down
to the bed, while awake desires
to pull me from the mattress,

force me to drink cups of coffee.
News launches from the TV,
showing disaster everywhere
which promises to visit me soon.

Shoes love my feet. The coat
sticks to my body. I swear
at late for pushing me out,
wave bye to early, on-time.

As I walk to work the cloud
of language hovers around me.
They're flies that summon firing,
fear, and anxiety, each one leaving

a nasty bite. I pick out hope,
but she's the least of her siblings.
"You have to really believe in me
for it to work." I chant her name.

I believe, I tell her, I believe.
She floats ahead of me, glowing.
She promises I'll get through this.

House

When I first saw my house on stilts,
running away like this was a track meet,
I didn't worry about a family member
being inside, or wonder about how it
obtained the stilts. I was disappointed
that it had decided to run away from us,
as if we were bad owners who bashed
in its walls or sent junk to the basement.

Yet, it must be our fault. I chased after it,
begging that we'd change, lay a fresh
coat of paint every year, ensure a roof
that would protect it from anything falling.
As it pounded through the streets,
evading traffic, it trailed wires and pipes,
shook off debris of masonry and wood.
I could see that it was headed to the sea,
and I imagined it stepping into waves,
waiting for the sea to swallow it up.

I shouted at it that it was my only home,
I forsook all others, as if we were married,
as if an owner was a spouse and lover.
It made it almost down to its door-frame,
when it sighed, I could swear it sighed,
and headed back to my plot of land,
as if it couldn't be Godzilla and return
to the ocean. Things changed then.

I spent all my weekends making sure
that everything sparkled in the kitchen,
that the plumbing was unclogged,
that the lawn was manicured perfectly.
Still, we were afraid of our domicile,
that it might choose to leave at night,
gently shaking us to the ground, where
we'd sleep peacefully as it drowned.

All That Happened

It began when I was small,
ended when I was much larger.
You could hardly see me
through a microscope, then
only through a telescope.
Yesterday I was a sliver,
then I became the moon.
Yesterday I was a point,
then I formed everything.
In between there were treasure
chests, eyeballs, spaceships.
Ghosts and pickled eggs.
In between there were martinis
and olives. Totalities, existences.
I could remember what happened.
I could never recall it all.

Road, Sky

You, the road, bend through the forest,
stab into the black hills, meet the sky.
The sky falls from outer space, leaves

the moon, the sun, drops to the road.
When sky meets road, you're worn,
you're half-broken, half-delighted,

traveled upon, asphalt in your lungs,
traffic lights studding your bones.
The sky washes each room of your house,

scrubbing toilets with clouds, peeling
away the green gunk inside your heart.
You want to keep moving forward,

for the stars to create a radiant trail
you can follow into their beauty.
The sky remains opposed to you,

forms a barrier you can't penetrate.
A wall that's nothing but red lights.
You must never change your life.

The Moon Is Up

I left for work with the moon still up.
I thought I should say something to it,
praise for staying up late so long, confusion

for wondering why it hadn't retired yet.
The buildings were wreathed in fading
darkness, the windows portholes to light.

Traffic ran as usual, speedy beetles
exiting, entering streets, imparting noise
of their farewells, exhaust and silence

when they departed. The gray mums died
next to the sidewalk. The puddles left
the path, the clouds taking the water.

Only a little mud touched the grass,
which was still bright green, despite Fall,
despite leaves collapsing on the ground.

If I could I'd build a miniature model
of this little world. I'd plant myself
in the middle, hands reaching out

toward the sky, as if I could change things
by praying to the blackness above me.
Except, it was a work day, and dreams

of holding everything in my hands
were illusory. Here was my brown desk,
my monitor, my keyboard. I was the action

figure typing up a memo. Watching
the sun come back through the blinds,
feeling I was heroic just being there.

The Universe

Everything we say about it is wrong:
it loves wet kisses, cuddles galaxies
around us, finds reasons to give hope
against entropy.

Last year we hated it,
called black holes its brains,
the constellations pretty dresses
that couldn't conceal that it
was an ugly pageant contestant after all.
Don't blame it if it compacts us,
dwindling down until all we can say is:
Get us off this tiny island.

If we were to be honest, we'd say
we deserve anything that happens:
we who took chances
on not smelling the roses,
hammering our heads into desks
until the surroundings didn't change
but we did: grabbing stars,
harassing huge fistfuls of night.

Hail Music

The hail made a kind of music we danced to.
Sometimes a swing tune, other times pop songs.
None of us wanted it to end, as we learned new

dances, ways to gyrate our skinny bodies.
We didn't fear its pounding, or the storm's
movement over the suburbs. Our roof was strong.

The trees would stand still like stone statues.
The only thing left to do was sing, to tell clouds
we were happy with disaster, loved crashing

ice. Our parents had different opinions.
They didn't understand this music, begging us
to come in to the basement, immerse ourselves

in tents and sleeping bags. No reason to feed
lives to destruction that wouldn't appreciate them.
In the end we obeyed them, left our fun.

The wind died down, leaving only small breezes
and dear pieces of hail. We tasted them.

Reservoir

I swim through the reservoir
and the fish die with me.
Cold metal taste in my mouth,
the current dragging me along.
While the trout and sunfish
can't find food, or become it.
I don't know what my heart
is doing, whether it'll betray me,
whether it doesn't know my breath.
Stroke, from the beginning, stroke
into the sun, away from land.
My fishing gear left, my clothes
sunning on shore, my own ghost.
Will they find me at the bottom?
Or bobbing next to reeds, glowing
with the rays, befriending grass
and weeds, the numerous animals?
I pray it will not be a child
who tries to fish me out with a stick.
That a grown-up turns him away,
the boy who is learning death.
I last recall being on the highway,
drinking beer after beer, seeing
the heat mirage on the blacktop.
This is me, the illusion. Everyone
believed I was here when I was not.

Surgery

I wear my scrubs to the living room.
I'm here to reconnect two arteries,
a passage between husband and wife.

It will take an unknown amount
of time. Instruments lie on the table:
kind words, honesty, forgiveness.

I open her mouth and she says,
"Why aren't things the way they were?"
A tap on the face and he says, "I

thought everything was all right with us."
Between their flow of words,
I cut into the red pulse of language.

Through "Everything she does hurts me,"
to "I don't understand what he's thinking."
When I discover the argument's heart,

beating roughly under skin, I know
what I must do to help them.
I let each of them touch the organ.

If they decide to let it fall, the burst
of a balloon, it's over. If they bring it
to their mouths, there is life. Still, life.

We Tried to Surrender to the Bus Driver

He just wanted change, for us to swipe
our fare-cards across an electronic surface.
Nobody on the vehicle would let us

give up. Nobody owned handcuffs
to take us away, or a phone to call law
enforcement, so they could drag us in.

When we got off, we encountered
a delivery person who refused to ship us
to the authorities, and a green grocer

who gave us a banana because she felt
sorry for us. When we woke this morning,
we had the feeling that we were guilty,

an imperative that we be captured
before we did any more harm. We
couldn't say what we'd done, or to whom

we'd done it to. Everything was shadowy,
reinforcing the absence of light. Finally,
we met our loves, who secured us in cars,

drove us around in circles so we'd
get confused, as they'd blindfolded us.
When we were led to the door, we

suspected a shark tank, or a meat grinder.
When we saw lights on the cakes, we knew
we'd been born. Frosting would stick

to our lips, the balloons would float
above us, red and bright like cherries
spinning in slot machines, dazzling in rows.

Jeff

Jeff was my mechanic, prone to lying,
but capable of repairing my engine, dents,

my inner life. Another Jeff was on signs
for elections, to lower taxes, put bad guys

in jail. He approved his TV commercials
with a zombie grin. Three Jeffs hid behind

the school, smoked pot, each one voiceless
except to say this was *very strong shit*.

They would catapult their station wagon
off a bridge, to be known as Jeff's bridge

by those who knew them. Jeff rung up
my *Penthouse* magazines without a wink.

Jeff sung at church without a lick of melody.
Some Jeffs in my city had a club,

deep in the financial district. where they
drank highballs, puffed cigars, decided

the direction of the world. I wanted to be
a Jeff. I slid myself to the city court

to fill in that name over mine,
but the judge wouldn't hear of it, slamming

his gavel. He spat tobacco at a spittoon,
questioned my manhood. All I desired

was a different life. How was that wrong?
The Jeffs above probably knew why,

gods dining on ambrosia, trucker caps on,
ready to ride their lightning down to my heart.

The Morning of the Scissors

The morning of the scissors is a welcome one.
It's time to cut out the moon above us,
leaving only light. It's our chance to eat stars
before they commit the crimes we wanted to.
Our belief is that the blades will perform
the procedures we have put off for too long.
They will conquer every shred of paper here,
filling the world with bits of white and black.
They will live a life beyond them, the nose
of the resurrected, the smile of blue razors.
Soon it will be noon and they will have to rest.
To lie in the drawer with other utensils
that have not done enough to earn their roles.
All around the desk are the shreds love
asked for—the notes without the words,
just alphabets without a ladder home
to the lips that kissed them, sent them away
with a wish to push the adored one step closer.
Now the path has been ripped. Nowhere to go,
nothing to do but forget language exists.
The heart of the "i" has been chipped and chewed.
It hangs off the ceiling lamp, slowly burning.

How the Moose Fell in Snow

You said something,
then I said something.
You wanted to talk
about moose, their habitat,
how you hunted them,
what their antlers looked like.
I wished to discuss
eternity, its nature, how
everything might not last
that long, how you and I
had souls, maybe eternal.
You changed the subject
to snack cakes, types
and sweetness, how
they were addictive,
how you dreamed of them,
how they made your wife
upset. I remarked
about death: who is he,
why is he cutting us down,
how can we beat him
and live forever and ever?
I mentioned to you
how the moose fell in snow,
blood on their heads.
How your cakes couldn't
bribe the Reaper.
You turned around and left.
It was a foul, overcast day.
In conditions like these,
we could choose
to believe in anything.

When She's Out

The universe has a personal discussion group
with yourself about how you will tell her
and when. The clock enters and exits time

often enough that you believe life has sped up,
that you will meet yourself from the other direction,
and that you will both argue and disagree.

The bed stays a bed, keeping its mattress content,
while the blankets pretend to be mountains,
and the pillow the white sighting of the moon.

A mirror wants to betray its sole occupation,
reflect back its glitzy surface instead of faces
with zits, the eye-patch on the middle aged

woman who'd had an operation, yellow teeth
that are no longer a secret of the mouth.
Even the tables and chairs don't wish to be

sat on or written on, their days of servitude
not behind them no matter what they think.
It's the lamp that misses her, as only another

source of light in the room would. It wrestles
the darkness of the hotel room to a standstill,
performs a victory lap around the pearly sink

and glassy TV, where no eye is shaded in night.
And it's the microwave that makes bad jokes
about her constant heating of tea, when she's

more than caffeinated enough, and what she wants
is you holding her wrist, feeling her pulse race,
everyone behind her in the marathon of love.

Horses

Horses stood in my living room,
not waiting to be ridden.

They watched TV, surfed the Web,
smoked cigarettes without an ashtray.

I wanted to saddle them all,
but their hooves promised to stomp me.

They wished to chomp my hands.
So I pulled the furniture outside.

I sat in an easy chair looking
at the moon, watched through

my telescope the friendliest stars.
The horses galloped upstairs, trying

to peer out windows at what I viewed.
They couldn't imagine the universe.

All they recalled was running
over plains, free from captivity.

How their legs were pure motion,
how their manes flew in the air.

Celestial Strut

O heaven, what could be worse
but your fabric promise,
your silky robes, your living wings.
Wouldn't we rather wear leather
jackets, studded jeans, a bandanna?
We'd be the tough cherubs,
the angry seraphim. God
would threaten to banish us,
tossing us out like a foam football,
for no one to dare catch, to watch
bounce on the ground.
We wouldn't fear him at all.
We'd strut through our future
celestial lovers. Our hands
would grip whatever brought us
pleasure. Our tongues would slash
ears, paint their faces with blue saliva.
The clouds around us would be too shy
to look. The pearly gates would shiver
with each glittery touch of the moon.

The Team

I slid home last night, though the field was wet,
and the bright lights killed any stars above.
The team gathered around me and lifted me
over their heads, as the dugout erupted
with music, a celebratory song I heard
many times in the past, and I tried to remember
the words so they would always stay with me.

But they didn't let me down, even after
the presentation of the trophies, and I asked them
to lower me to the ground. They went home
with me, my wife greeting each one slapping
their hands, serving all the beer in the fridge.
Then they all entered my shower, where water
sprayed on us, and they soaped everybody.

Later, the crowd gathered around my love,
who had put on expensive lingerie, sprayed
French perfume, and I couldn't see what they
were doing, but a combination of moans
and "More!" spurred me to scramble off
the group. But they wouldn't let me exit
their hands, even as the noise reached a crescendo,
even as I feared the worse. Then they slept
in a large heap, my head still rising above them.

When they woke in the morning, they shoved me
inside a box, nailed it shut. I heard them singing
New Orleans blues songs, and a jazz band ran behind
the procession. There, the mourners became one
groaning mouth and tongue. The minister, who was
really five ministers, told the world what a great man
I was, and how this burial was the only possible end.

Then the team traveled into the hole with me,
and let dirt fall around them, while I heard
the cheers we started with. How amazing
it was to be pushed upward by limbs, how
their fingers were beautiful, how their hands
and their warmth would never leave.

The Art of Dissolving

What you have to do is think
of Alka-Seltzers, those speckled pills
splashing into a glass like bank robbers

falling from a cliff, which foam,
bubble when they hit the water.
When it's time to be devoured

you can walk away from your job,
hear those plops in your mind as you
walk around with your personal box

of effects, feel your legs, stomach,
chest start to explode with fizz,
while your head readies itself to drop,

lose all the thoughts you ever had.
But "Oh, what a relief it is!" not to have
them, to wander underground in the life

of the mind, where no one suspects
you haven't been spent, dissolved
so the world can drink you quicker.

Misdirection

It doesn't have to be a crime.
You could replace
your spouse's light yogurt
with regular flavored.
Or give someone wrong directions,
so she ends up
in the warehouse district.
Even set up a fake store
where people can buy make-believe
products, each one
—horse jam, octopus wine,
butter made of politicians—
more ridiculous than the next.
It can be a little trick,
a kind of misdirection.
Like love—
you can stay with a person
a full 40 years
and say at the last
that it wasn't true.
All the joy and pain was plastic,
all the laughter and tears
were lies. Watch
your graves split apart.
Watch the sorrow
on the gravedigger's
smile.

Donald Illich was born in Biloxi, Mississippi. He received a bachelor's degree in journalism from Ohio University and a master's degree in literature from Illinois State University. At OU he studied writing with Wayne Dodd and Eve Shelnutt, and at ISU he studied writing with David Foster Wallace and Curtis White.

He is President of The Federal Poets, a long-running poetry workshop group in Washington, D.C. He has read his poetry widely in D.C., Virginia, and Maryland, including at the Iota Club Reading Series, Café Muse, Kensington Row Bookshop Reading Series, and the Evil Grin Reading Series. He has published poetry in many literary journals, including *Iowa Review, LIT, Nimrod, Passages North, Rattle, Cream City Review, Crab Creek Review, St. Petersburg Review, Waccamaw, Gravel, Bodega, Sink Review,* and *No Tell Motel.*

He works as a technical writer-editor for the Federal government. He lives in Rockville, Maryland, with his wife Julia.

www.ingramcontent.com/pod-product-compliance
Lightning Source LLC
LaVergne TN
LVHW041517070426
835507LV00012B/1638